MONEY

Knows Your Name

A 30-DAY DIVINE
WEALTH DEVOTIONAL

Frank C. Delaney
Author

Money Knows Your Name by Frank C. Delaney

All Scripture quotations, unless otherwise indicated, are taken from the King James Version®.

Introduction

Glory to God! I am so excited that you have collided with increase. "Money Knows My Name" is a prophetic release and overflow from what has been imparted, tried and proven in my own personal life. The word of God declares that They overcame him by the blood of the lamb and the words of their testimony. This devotional is a testament of what has become a consistent in my life. I am a living witness that "Money Knows My Name", yes it follows me, it finds me, it is attracted to me!

One day I decided to develop a relationship with the biblical principles of wealth. I gained an understanding of what God's word had to say about wealth, not money, but wealth. I learned that the process of prosperity is one that must also be tried and proven. I have many moments and memories that I could share on my journey to becoming acquainted with wealth, which brings money.

"Money Knows My Name', is answered assignment and mandate to elevate lives and to provide a tool that will create a rich, godly relationship with money. Let's Go!!!

Day 1

See IT...Speak IT...Believe IT
Receive IT!

---

[18] But thou shalt remember the Lord thy God: for it is he that giveth thee power to get wealth, that he may establish his covenant which he swore unto thy fathers, as it is this day.

Deuteronomy 8:18(KJV)

My passion is helping people
I love to teach a thing
taking care of ppl. I
love seeing PP HAPPY

Confess

This is the day the Father is giving you power to dominant in the area of the Marketplace. He is releasing, concepts, contacts, contracts, and checks. Look up He's giving you the power (idea/concepts) to get wealth. This is a covenant that has already been established. Take a moment and write out what you're passionate about and watch the Father reveal power to get wealth.

Declare

Money, you know my name, come to me NOW!
Money thou are loosed in Jesus Name!

Say it again at 4pm your time. This is the 8 watch of Prayer. The eight watches of prayer open a portal for the universe to respond.

You Decree

Money you know my name. I decree multiple concepts to get wealth I shall be the lender & not the borrow.

Day 2

See IT...Speak IT...Believe IT
Receive IT!

---

^{18} Let them shout for joy, and be glad, that favour my righteous cause: yea, let them say continually, Let the Lord be magnified, which hath pleasure in the prosperity of his servant.

Psalm 35:27(KJV)

Confess

Favour is getting ready to consume me like fire! Stop

right now and...Give Abba praise for the favor that is

getting ready to hit your life, family, job, ministry,

business and whatever else you desire.

Declare

Money, you know my name, come to me NOW!
Money thou are loosed in Jesus Name!

Say it again at 4pm your time. This is the 8 watch of Prayer. The eight watches of prayer open a portal for the universe to respond.

You Decree

I decree I live in wealth
I live on top. I have
more than enough

Day 3

See IT...Speak IT...Believe IT
Receive IT!

---

[26] For God giveth to a man that is good in his sight wisdom, and knowledge, and joy: but to the sinner he giveth travail, to gather and to heap up, that he may give to him that is good before God.

Ecclesiastes 2:26(KJV)

Confess

The word of God declares that wisdom is the principle thing. Today, begin to praise God for His divine wisdom and principles of increase and establishment.

Declare

Money, you know my name, come to me NOW!
Money thou are loosed in Jesus Name!

Say it again at 4pm your time. This is the 8 watch of Prayer. The eight watches of prayer open a portal for the universe to respond.

You Decree

New Ideas to advance the Kingdom.
Money is supernaturaley deposited
into my Captial One acct in 4764

Day 4

See IT...Speak IT...Believe IT
Receive IT!

─────────────────

[4] Delight thyself also in the Lord: and he shall give thee the desires of thine heart.[5] Commit thy way unto the Lord; trust also in him; and he shall bring it to pass.

Psalm 37:4-5(KJV)

Confess

Today, I commit my way unto you Lord. I trust that

my delight in him shall manifest divine prosperity and

increase.

Declare

Money, you know my name, come to me NOW!
Money thou are loosed in Jesus Name!

Say it again at 4pm your time. This is the 8 watch of Prayer. The eight watches of prayer open a portal for the universe to respond.

You Decree

I will commit my way to the Lord
I shall see the manifestation of
divine prosperity. I will delight in
Him.

Day 5

See IT...Speak IT...Believe IT
Receive IT!

---

[38] Give, and it shall be given unto you; good measure, pressed down, and shaken together, and running over, shall men give into your bosom. For with the same measure that ye mete withal it shall be measured to you again.

Luke 6:38(KJV)

Confess

A tsunami of increase shall be my measure this day, because of threefold seed that of time, talent and treasure. The seed shall reproduce and yield a plentiful harvest in Jesus name.

Declare

Money, you know my name, come to me NOW!
Money thou are loosed in Jesus Name!

Say it again at 4pm your time. This is the 8 watch of Prayer. The eight watches of prayer open a portal for the universe to respond.

You Decree

Money you know my name. I have
because I always give.
I am a money magnet I am a
favor magnet.

Day 6

See IT...Speak IT...Believe IT
Receive IT!

---

[6] In the house of the righteous is much treasure: but in the revenues of the wicked is trouble.

Proverbs 15:6 (KJV)

Confess

I shall withhold my righteousness and preserve

revenue for peace. Peace that shall lead to prosperous

waters that flow.

Declare

Money, you know my name, come to me NOW!
Money thou are loosed in Jesus Name!

*Say it again at 4pm your time. This is the 8 watch of
Prayer. The eight watches of prayer open a portal for
the universe to respond.*

You Decree

Debt Freedom Romans 8:28

I Decree a Eph 3:20 over my life.

Day 7

See IT...Speak IT...Believe IT
Receive IT!

---

[4] By humility and the fear of the Lord are riches, and honour, and life.

Proverbs 22:4(KJV)

Confess

This next level of honor and riches is being release into my life because of my humility and reverence for the Lord.

Declare

Money, you know my name, come to me NOW!
Money thou are loosed in Jesus Name!

Say it again at 4pm your time. This is the 8 watch of Prayer. The eight watches of prayer open a portal for the universe to respond.

You Decree

_____

_____

_____

Day 8

See IT...Speak IT...Believe IT
Receive IT!

---

[6] But without faith it is impossible to please him: for he that cometh to God must believe that he is, and that he is a rewarder of them that diligently seek him.

Hebrews 11:6 (KJV)

Confess
My faith and diligence shall produce a seek of

prosperity that will tend roots and wells of reward.

Declare
Money, you know my name, come to me NOW!
Money thou are loosed in Jesus Name!

Say it again at 4pm your time. This is the 8 watch of Prayer. The eight watches of prayer open a portal for the universe to respond.

You Decree

_____

_____

_____

Day 9

See IT...Speak IT...Believe IT
Receive IT!

---

21 That I may cause those that love me to inherit substance; and I will fill their treasures.

Proverbs 8:21(KJV)

Confess

I stand in the gap today for others, that the overflow of my substance shall be available to them that are in divine alignment.

Declare

Money, you know my name, come to me NOW!
Money thou are loosed in Jesus Name!

Say it again at 4pm your time. This is the 8 watch of Prayer. The eight watches of prayer open a portal for the universe to respond.

You Decree

_____

_____

_____

Day 10

See IT...Speak IT...Believe IT
Receive IT!

---

²¹ That If you be willing and obedient you shall eat the good of the land.

Isaiah 1:19(KJV)

Confess

My obedience to eat the Word of God concerning prosperity and increase is changing my taste buds for wealth.

Declare

Money, you know my name, come to me NOW!
Money thou are loosed in Jesus Name!

Say it again at 4pm your time. This is the 8 watch of Prayer. The eight watches of prayer open a portal for the universe to respond.

You Decree

_____

_____

_____

Day 11

See IT...Speak IT...Believe IT
Receive IT!

---

[11] Cast thy bread upon the waters: for thou shalt find it after many days.

Ecclesiastes 11:1(KJV)

Confess

I shall sacrifice the fullness of my belly to obtain the

reward of prosperity, that floweth like a river.

Declare

Money, you know my name, come to me NOW!
Money thou are loosed in Jesus Name!

Say it again at 4pm your time. This is the 8 watch of Prayer. The eight watches of prayer open a portal for the universe to respond.

You Decree

_____

_____

_____

Day 12

See IT...Speak IT...Believe IT
Receive IT!

---

[19] Blessed be the Lord, who daily loadeth us with benefits, even the God of our salvation. Selah.

Psalm 68:19(KJV)

Confess

I am overflowing with grace because of God's benefits in my life. I receive the benefits of prosperity and give honor to the God of my salvation.

Declare

Money, you know my name, come to me NOW!
Money thou are loosed in Jesus Name!

Say it again at 4pm your time. This is the 8 watch of Prayer. The eight watches of prayer open a portal for the universe to respond.

You Decree

_____

_____

_____

Day 13

See IT...Speak IT...Believe IT
Receive IT!

———————————————————————

[3] Wealth and riches shall be in his house: and his righteousness endureth forever.

Psalm 112:3(KJV)

Confess

Wealth and riches is my inheritance. The Lord has declared that the surplus shall be in my house.

Declare

Money, you know my name, come to me NOW!
Money thou are loosed in Jesus Name!

Say it again at 4pm your time. This is the 8 watch of Prayer. The eight watches of prayer open a portal for the universe to respond.

You Decree

_____

_____

_____

Day 14

See IT...Speak IT...Believe IT
Receive IT!

---

[10] Bring ye all the tithes into the storehouse, that there may be meat in mine house, and prove me now herewith, saith the Lord of hosts, if I will not open you the windows of heaven, and pour you out a blessing, that there shall not be room enough to receive it.

Malachi 3:10(KJV)

Confess

My tithe is my obedience that grants me access to the storehouse of increase and overflowing blessings.

Declare

Money, you know my name, come to me NOW!
Money thou are loosed in Jesus Name!

Say it again at 4pm your time. This is the 8 watch of Prayer. The eight watches of prayer open a portal for the universe to respond.

You Decree

_____

_____

_____

Day 15

See IT...Speak IT...Believe IT
Receive IT!

---

⁷ For your shame ye shall have double; and for confusion they shall rejoice in their portion: therefore, in their land they shall possess the double: everlasting joy shall be unto them.

Isaiah 61:7(KJV)

Confess

Double is my portion in Jesus Name!

Double is my portion in Jesus Name!

Double is my portion in Jesus Name!

Declare

Money, you know my name, come to me NOW!
Money thou are loosed in Jesus Name!

Say it again at 4pm your time. This is the 8 watch of Prayer. The eight watches of prayer open a portal for the universe to respond.

Decree

_____

_____

_____

Day 16

See IT...Speak IT...Believe IT
Receive IT!

---

¹⁹ Every man also to whom God hath given riches and wealth, and hath given him power to eat thereof, and to take his portion, and to rejoice in his labour; this is the gift of God.

Ecclesiastes 5:19(KJV))

Confess
Riches and Wealth are granted by God according to thy labour. I'm thankful that my portion has been established in His gift.

Declare
Money, you know my name, come to me NOW!
Money thou are loosed in Jesus Name!

Say it again at 4pm your time. This is the 8 watch of Prayer. The eight watches of prayer open a portal for the universe to respond.

You Decree

_____

_____

_____

Day 17

See IT...Speak IT...Believe IT
Receive IT!

---

²⁵ Save now, I beseech thee, O Lord: O Lord, I beseech thee, send now prosperity.

Psalm 118:25(KJV))

Confess

Lord your prosperity cometh to save them that hearken to your will. Today I hearken, I hear and I herald your word to rise in increase.

Declare

Money, you know my name, come to me NOW!
Money thou are loosed in Jesus Name!

Say it again at 4pm your time. This is the 8 watch of Prayer. The eight watches of prayer open a portal for the universe to respond.

You Decree

_____

_____

_____

Day 18

See IT...Speak IT...Believe IT
Receive IT!

---

[10] The young lions do lack, and suffer hunger: but they that seek the Lord shall not want any good thing.

Psalm 34:10(KJV))

Confess

I am a seeker and the seeker shall not lack. I thank God today that the seekers shall increase in wealth and prosperity according to His will and His way.

Declare

Money, you know my name, come to me NOW!
Money thou are loosed in Jesus Name!

Say it again at 4pm your time. This is the 8 watch of Prayer. The eight watches of prayer open a portal for the universe to respond.

You Decree

_____

_____

_____

Day 19

See IT...Speak IT...Believe IT
Receive IT!

---

¹⁴ The Lord shall increase you more and more, you and your children.

Psalm 115:14(KJV))

Confess

This outpouring of increase that is hitting my life is not just falling upon me but on the generations before me and after me. The moment of increase is hitting those connected to my destiny and spiritual DNA. Increase is flowing in my blood and theirs.

Declare

Money, you know my name, come to me NOW!
Money thou are loosed in Jesus Name!

Say it again at 4pm your time. This is the 8 watch of Prayer. The eight watches of prayer open a portal for the universe to respond.

You Decree

_____

_____

_____

Day 20

See IT...Speak IT...Believe IT
Receive IT!

---

[6] Pray for the peace of Jerusalem: they shall prosper that love thee.

[7] Peace be within thy walls, and prosperity within thy palaces.

Psalm 122:6-7(KJV))

<u>**Confess**</u>

My cry for Jerusalem is ushering me into a greater place of prosperity and peace. I want just walk in prosperity but I shall walk in peace.

Declare

Money, you know my name, come to me NOW!
Money thou are loosed in Jesus Name!

Say it again at 4pm your time. This is the 8 watch of Prayer. The eight watches of prayer open a portal for the universe to respond.

You Decree

_____

_____

_____

Day 21

See IT...Speak IT...Believe IT
Receive IT!

---

24 Therefore I say unto you, What things soever ye desire, when ye pray, believe that ye receive them, and ye shall have them.

Mark 11:24(KJV))

Confess

My prayer life is changing my financial trajectory. I am no longer walking in fear but faith. This is a divine moment in my life and I am embracing it to obtain my desires.

Declare

Money, you know my name, come to me NOW!
Money thou are loosed in Jesus Name!

Say it again at 4pm your time. This is the 8 watch of Prayer. The eight watches of prayer open a portal for the universe to respond.

You Decree

_____

_____

_____

Day 22

See IT...Speak IT...Believe IT
Receive IT!

---

22 The blessing of the Lord, it maketh rich, and he addeth no sorrow with it.

Proverbs 10:22(KJV))

Confess

The blessings of the Lord that are upon my life are impacting me for a greater place. I am no longer sad and emotional. I am walking in greater abilities of increase because the joy of the Lord and the blessings of the Lord are overwhelming me NO! SHOUT NOW! NOW...NO LACK...NO SORROW.

Declare

Money, you know my name, come to me NOW!
Money thou are loosed in Jesus Name!

Say it again at 4pm your time. This is the 8 watch of Prayer. The eight watches of prayer open a portal for the universe to respond.

You Decree

_____

_____

_____

Day 23

See IT...Speak IT...Believe IT
Receive IT!

---

23 The Lord is my shepherd; I shall not want.

Psalms 23:1(KJV))

Confess

My shepherd is Jehovah Jireh and I don't lack in anything. My dependence and trust upon Him is bringing me into a wealthy place.

Declare

Money, you know my name, come to me NOW!
Money thou are loosed in Jesus Name!

Say it again at 4pm your time. This is the 8 watch of Prayer. The eight watches of prayer open a portal for the universe to respond.

You Decree

_____

_____

_____

Day 24

See IT...Speak IT...Believe IT
Receive IT!

---

[19] But my God shall supply all your need according to his riches in glory by Christ Jesus.

Philippians 4:19(KJV))

Confess

My supplier has come and He is funding my future. He is not just taking care of my immediate needs but everything that has been predestined in my life.

Declare

Money, you know my name, come to me NOW!
Money thou are loosed in Jesus Name!

Say it again at 4pm your time. This is the 8 watch of Prayer. The eight watches of prayer open a portal for the universe to respond.

You Decree

_____

_____

_____

Day 25

See IT...Speak IT...Believe IT
Receive IT!

---

[7] Though thy beginning was small, yet thy latter end should greatly increase.

Job 8:7(KJV))

Confess

This Mega increase that is hitting my life is causing me to forget the small beginning that ever hit my life. The small beginnings in my life prepared me for what is greatly increasing NOW!

Declare

Money, you know my name, come to me NOW!
Money thou are loosed in Jesus Name!

Say it again at 4pm your time. This is the 8 watch of Prayer. The eight watches of prayer open a portal for the universe to respond.

You Decree

_____

_____

_____

Day 26

See IT...Speak IT...Believe IT
Receive IT!

---

[21] Thou shalt increase my greatness, and comfort me on every side.

Psalm 71:21(KJV))

Confess

This level of Increase is expanding my reach. It's causing me to flourish into the place of the known. I am moving from place of the unknown into the place of begin known in every area of kingdom societal influence. (Religion, Family, Education, government, media, arts &entertainment and business.)

Declare

Money, you know my name, come to me NOW! Money thou are loosed in Jesus Name!

Say it again at 4pm your time. This is the 8 watch of Prayer. The eight watches of prayer open a portal for the universe to respond.

You Decree

_____

_____

_____

Day 27

See IT...Speak IT...Believe IT
Receive IT!

---

[19] A feast is made for laughter, and wine maketh merry: but money answereth all things.

Ecclesiastes 10:19(KJV))

Confess

I am getting ready to experience a year of answers.

Money, is getting ready to flood my life like wine.

Wine is my portion this year. The wine of creativity is
entering my life in seven ways.

Declare

Money, you know my name, come to me NOW!
Money thou are loosed in Jesus Name!

*Say it again at 4pm your time. This is the 8 watch of
Prayer. The eight watches of prayer open a portal for
the universe to respond.*

You Decree

_____

_____

_____

Day 28

See IT...Speak IT...Believe IT
Receive IT!

---

⁹ Honour the Lord with thy substance, and with the first-fruits of all thine increase: ¹⁰ So shall thy barns be filled with plenty, and thy presses shall burst out with new wine.

Proverbs 3:9-10 (KJV))

Confess

I prophetically declare this scripture over your life today. "Yes indeed, it won't be long now." God's Decree. "Things are going to happen so fast your head will swim, one thing fast on the heels of the other. You won't be able to keep up. Everything will be happening at once—and everywhere you look, blessings! Blessings like wine pouring off the mountains and hills. I'll make everything right again for my people Israel.

Declare

Money, you know my name, come to me NOW!
Money thou are loosed in Jesus Name!

Say it again at 4pm your time. This is the 8 watch of Prayer. The eight watches of prayer open a portal for the universe to respond.

You Decree

_____

_____

_____

Day 29

See IT...Speak IT...Believe IT
Receive IT!

---

[12] Both riches and honour come of thee, and thou reignest over all; and in thine hand is power and might; and in thine hand it is to make great, and to give strength unto all.

I Chronicles 29:12 (KJV))

Confess

Riches and honor are due unto me. I am in a season of Honor. My season of Thank you and Congrats! The hour where people will bless me like crazy. Crazy favor is about to hit my life in an enormous way. The strength and power of the Lord is rising upon my life so that I can gain wealth in a phenomenal way. Riches and honor is falling upon me this week. I am Looking for it! I am Expecting it! It's due unto me.

Declare

Money, you know my name, come to me NOW!
Money thou are loosed in Jesus Name!

Say it again at 4pm your time. This is the 8 watch of Prayer. The eight watches of prayer open a portal for the universe to respond.

You Decree

_____

_____

_____

Day 30

See IT...Speak IT...Believe IT
Receive IT!

---

²² While the earth remaineth, seedtime and harvest, and cold and heat, and summer and winter, and day and night shall not cease.

Genesis 8:22 (KJV))

Confess

SHOUT! It's Harvest TIME! I have made it to my season of Harvest. My sowing and confession have not been in vain. My seeds have weathered the storm and now it's time to see total manifestation of my end time Harvest. I declare today that I am stepping in full authority to receive total manifestation of my seasons of sowing and NOW it's time for me to REAP A MAJOR HARVEST. I have made it to the place where I can declare

MONEY YOU KNOW <u>(your name here)</u>

come to ME NOW!

You Decree

_____

_____

_____

Made in the
USA
Columbia, SC